Contents

Ruth and Shushi love playing with water. Come and play with them!

Fill up the pool!

It's a hot day. Mum fills the paddling pool for Ruth and Shushi. The water sparkles in the sunshine.

We use water every day.

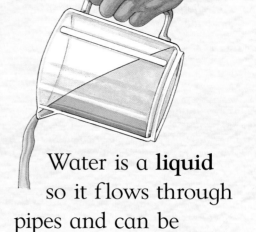

Water is a **liquid** so it flows through pipes and can be poured out of jugs.

Water is colourless, and has no smell.

In how many ways have you used water today?

6

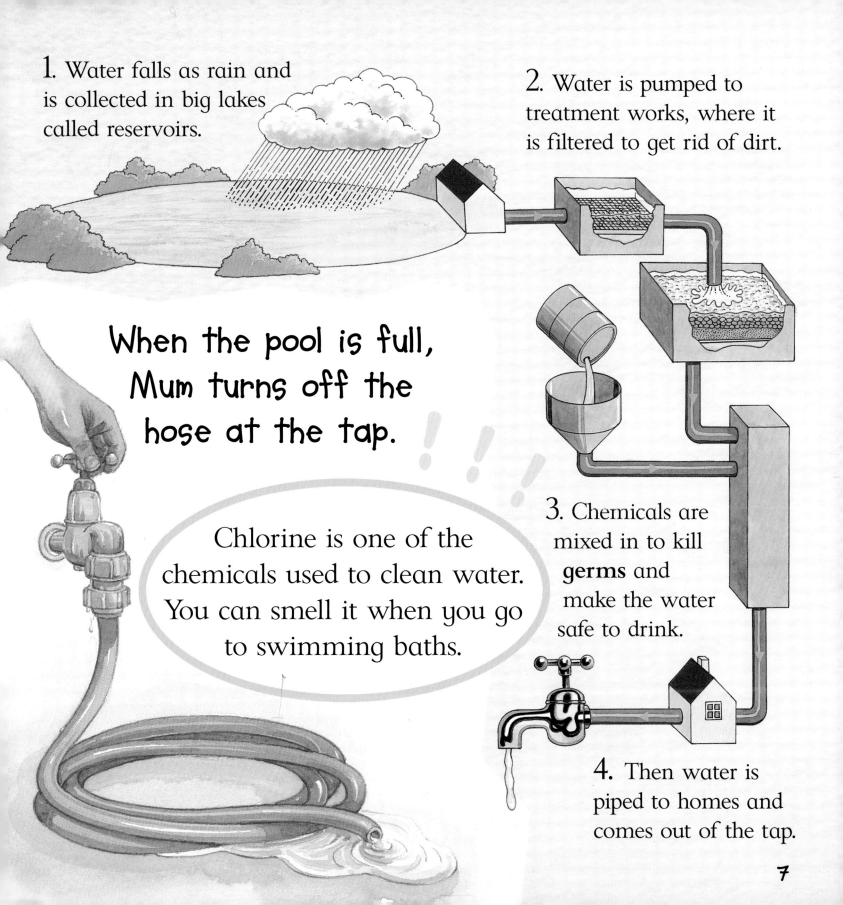

1. Water falls as rain and is collected in big lakes called reservoirs.

2. Water is pumped to treatment works, where it is filtered to get rid of dirt.

When the pool is full, Mum turns off the hose at the tap.

Chlorine is one of the chemicals used to clean water. You can smell it when you go to swimming baths.

3. Chemicals are mixed in to kill **germs** and make the water safe to drink.

4. Then water is piped to homes and comes out of the tap.

7

We use water for:

Drinking

Cooking

Swimming

Watering plants

The girls jump in the water. Mum has added drops of blue food colouring and soapy liquid for extra fun!

We get water by turning on the tap. It is clean and safe. In some countries, people have to walk many kilometres to collect safe water.

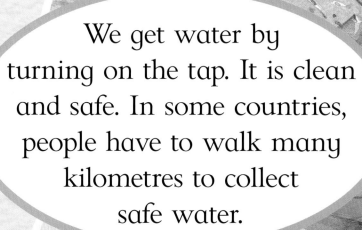

8

We use water mixed with soap for:

Washing away germs

Washing our bodies and hair

Washing clothes and dishes

Dirt sticks to soap. When you rinse away the soap with clean water, you wash away the dirt, too.

Blowing bubbles

Pouring water

Ruth and Shushi pour water from a jug into a bottle – and back again. The water changes its shape as it fills each container.

Water is a liquid, so it takes on the shape of the container it is poured into.

There is the same amount of coloured water in each of these three containers.

What happens to the shape of the water when you pour it from a long thin glass into a short, fat round one?

Now the girls are playing under the flower shower – and having a water fight!

Water flows in lots of different ways.

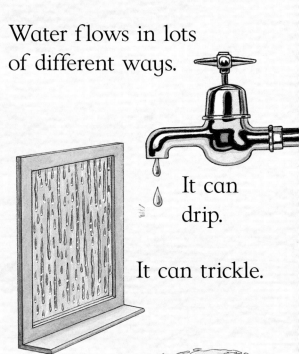

It can drip.

It can trickle.

It can swirl down the plughole.

It can squirt.

It can gush over a waterfall.

Some things float in water.

Plastic beaker

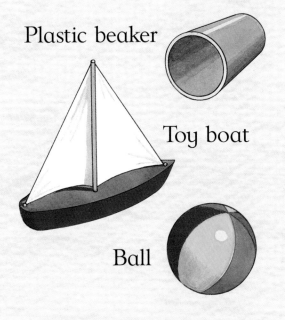

Toy boat

Ball

Some things sink.

Metal toy car

Pebble

Shell

Marble

It floats!

Ruth and Shushi are playing with toys in the water. Some float, but others sink.

Ruth floated a plastic beaker. Then she filled the beaker with water and tried again. What do you think happened?

Water pushes up on things. If the force of the water's push is strong enough, something floats.

Even a big metal boat floats because the force of the water pushing up is stronger than the boat pushing down.

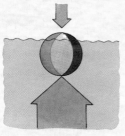 Try to push a ball underwater like Shushi, and feel the water pushing back.

Shushi pushes a ball under the water and then lets go. The ball whooshes back up into the air!

Why do you think the ball bobs back up to the surface of the water when Shushi lets go of it?

We're thirsty

The girls are hot and thirsty. Mum has mixed a fruit cordial with water for them to drink.

We are mostly made of water so we need to drink plenty every day to keep healthy.

We lose water as we:

Sweat

Go to the toilet

Cry

Breathe out

When our bodies need more water, we feel thirsty.

Have you ever noticed your breath misting a window? It is the water in your breath that makes the glass mist up!

You must be thirsty too, Bramble.

These plants will wilt in this heat without a drink.

Ruth gives the dog some water too. Mum waters the plants.

In dry weather, you can put water out for the birds. They like to drink it - and bath in it!

Just like us, animals need water to drink.

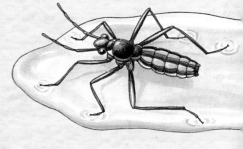

Plants need water to grow.

Water **freezes** to form **ice**. We see ice in the kitchen:

Ice cubes

Ice lollies

We see ice in nature:

Icicles

Frozen ponds

Snowflakes

Hail

When it warms up, ice **melts** to form water again.

Ice on a stick

Ruth's dad has bought the girls some ice lollies. Ruth and Shushi eat them quickly so they do not melt!

Food is sometimes frozen to make it last longer. It is the water in the food that freezes.

Dad has a drink instead. He puts ice cubes in it to cool it down.

What happens to water when it freezes?

It changes from a liquid to a **solid**.

It changes from clear to cloudy white.

Fill a plastic bottle half full of water and mark its level. Put it in a freezer until the water turns to ice. What is the level of the frozen water?

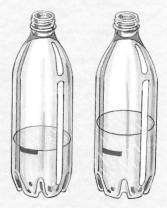

It takes up more space.

Down the drain

After eating the lollies, the girls wash their sticky hands in hot, soapy water. The dirty water swirls down the plughole.

How does the water get to the tap? Turn back to page 7 for help.

How does the water get to the tap? Turn back to page 7 for help.

1. The dirty water from our houses runs down pipes and into drains.

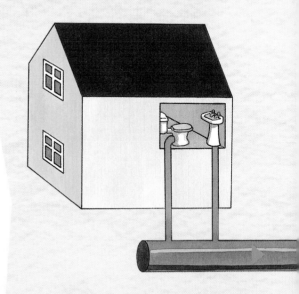

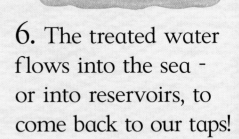

6. The treated water flows into the sea - or into reservoirs, to come back to our taps!

5. The water is cleaned further and chemicals are added to make it safe.

Ruth goes to the toilet and flushes the waste away. She washes her hands again.

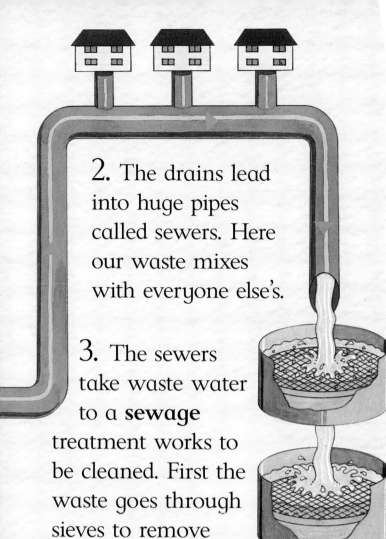

2. The drains lead into huge pipes called sewers. Here our waste mixes with everyone else's.

3. The sewers take waste water to a **sewage** treatment works to be cleaned. First the waste goes through sieves to remove large bits of dirt.

4. Next the dirty water stands in tanks. Slowly the sludgy waste drops to the bottom and the water trickles off again.

Everyone needs water. We use it carefully and recycle it to make sure there is enough to go round.

19

Materials are what things are made of.

Water cannot pass through some materials. These materials are **waterproof**.

Glass is waterproof. Windows keep out the rain.

Some clothes and boots are waterpoof. So are umbrellas!

Keeping dry

The girls want to play outside again – but the weather has changed. It's raining!

Ducks can play outside whatever the weather!

The girls watch the raindrops trickling down the windows.

Oil and water do not mix together, so oily coatings make things waterproof.

Birds make a special oil which they spread over their feathers to keep dry.

Wood can soak up water. We use paint made from oil to make it waterproof.

Pour some cooking oil onto some water in a glass. What happens? Try mixing it together. What happens now?

When water is heated, it starts to bubble gently.

As it gets hotter, it bubbles fiercely. We say it **boils**.

When water boils, it changes from a liquid to a **gas** called **steam**. Steam rises from the boiling water.

Hot drinks

As the rain keeps falling, Mum puts the kettle on for hot drinks – and fills the kitchen with steam.

Steam is boiling hot. Never put your hand near where the steam comes out of a boiling kettle or pan.

22

When steam cools, it changes back to liquid water again.

When hot steam hits a cold window, it forms lots of little water droplets.

Sometimes windows steam up just because the weather is damp and cold. There is always some water in the air.

The kitchen windows have steamed up. Ruth and Shushi draw smiley faces on the damp glass.

23

When you mix some things with water, they seem to disappear. We say they **dissolve**. Here are some things that dissolve.

Salt

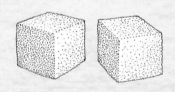
Sugar

Instant coffee

Chemicals in tap water

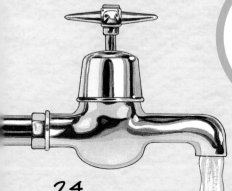

Dad makes the drinks. He and Mum have coffee. Mum stirs some sugar into her mug.

Add one teaspoon of sugar to a cup of cold water and one teaspoon to the same amount of warm water. Does the sugar dissolve more easily in warm water?

Shushi and Ruth have hot chocolate with marshmallows! They're painting a 'rainy day' picture.

Some things do not dissolve in water.

Flour

Paint powder

Sand

Hot chocolate powder

When you rinse your paint brushes in water, what happens if you leave the water standing for a day?

A dishwasher

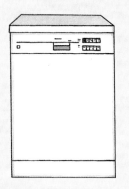

Water everywhere

It's time for Shushi to go home.
She's enjoyed playing with water.
What would we do without water?
We use it every day!

A washing
machine

Can you find these
things in Ruth's
kitchen? How do they
use water?

A vase
of flowers

Some paints

A kettle

An ice tray

Can you find some steam and some ice in the picture? How are they different from liquid water?

A hamster

A sauce pan

A water pistol

Try this yourself

Have some fun with water.

Talcum powder swirly

Discover which way water swirls when it goes down the plughole.

1. Fill a sink with water.
2. Shake talcum powder on the surface of the water.
3. Pull out the plug!
4. Watch what happens. Which way round does the water swirl?
5. Try this several times. Does it always swirl the same way?

Be a Water Wizard!

This 'science trick' will surprise your friends - and even your parents! You need a fresh egg, two bowls of water (one warm, one cold), some salt and a spoon.

1. Add the salt a little at a time to the bowl of warm water and stir until it dissolves. Keep on adding salt until it stops dissolving. Let the water cool.
2. Hide the salt and the spoon!
3. Take the other bowl of water and ask your friends or parents to try to float an egg in it. The egg will sink!
4. Take the egg from them, and pretend to 'cast a spell' on the bowl of salty water. Then put the egg in the water and, hey presto, it floats! It's the salt in the water that helps the egg float.

Floating and sinking

Use two large balls of Plasticine, about the size of tennis balls, to experiment more with floating and sinking.

1. Put the balls of Plasticine into a bowl of water. Do they sink or float?
2. Take one ball out of the water and make a boat shape with high sides.
3. Put it in the water. Does it float? If not, adjust the shape until it does.

4. Once you've made a boat that floats, vary the shape. Make a boat with high sides and a small bottom, and a boat with low sides and a large, flat bottom. Which shape floats best?

Useful words

boil: To heat a liquid to the point where it bubbles and changes into a gas.

dissolve: To mix a solid with water so it seems to disappear.

freeze: To cool a liquid so it changes to a solid.

gas: Some materials are gases. The air we breathe is a mixture of gases. Steam is a gas.

germs: Tiny living things that can make us ill.

ice: Frozen water.

liquid: Some materials are liquids. Water is a liquid. It can be poured and takes the shape of the container it is held in.

materials: Materials are what things are made of.

melt: To heat a solid so it changes to a liquid.

sewage: The dirty waste water that runs from sinks, baths and toilets into drains and sewers.

solid: Some materials are solids. They have their own shape. Ice is a solid.

steam: The gas water becomes when you boil it.

waterproof: Water cannot pass through a waterproof material.

About this book

This book encourages children to explore and discover science in their local, familiar environment - in the home or school, garden or park. By starting from 'where they are', it aims to increase children's knowledge and understanding of the world around them, encouraging them to examine objects and living things closely and from a more scientific perspective.

Water and its uses are examined, along with floating and sinking. The way water is found in all three different states is also introduced. All this is done using 'child friendly' terms and questions that build on children's natural curiosity and encourage them to think for themselves. The aim is to lay a strong foundation for the reader's future, more complex, learning in science.

Index